walk with me.
a sister's story

a guided journal of memories
to share with my sibling

Other Books In The "Walk With Me" Series:

A Great-Grandmother's Story
A Great-Grandfather's Story
A Grandmother's Story
A Grandfather's Story
A Mother's Story
A Father's Story
A Stepmother's Story
A Stepfather's Story

wandering tortoise

Copyright 2020 Patricia N. Hicks.
Includes licensed art by Molly Van Roekel.
All rights reserved.

No part of this publication may be reproduced, distributed or transmitted
in any form or by any means, including photocopying, recording,
or other electronic or mechanical methods, without prior
written permission of the author, except as permitted by US copyright law.

ISBN: 979-8620700356

Introduction

Dear Sister,
This guided journal is a fantastic way to create a
one-of-a-kind record of
the events, circumstances and defining moments
that molded and shaped you into the person you are today.
Share your innermost hopes and dreams
and the fascinating stories of your life on these pages.

Includes 101 thought-provoking writing prompts
written from the perspective of your sibling.
Write as though you are speaking directly to them.

You can choose to complete one page a day or several at once.
Pages can be completed in any order you desire.

There are plenty of places for writing, but there are also
empty pages at the beginning of each section that can be
filled with photographs, clippings, and anything else you wish
to include to help bring your stories to life.

The Sibling Relationship

The Real You

Life

Your Full Name

Your Date of Birth

Your Place of Birth

the date you began this journal

the person you are completing this journal for

The Sibling Relationship

What do you like about being a sister? What do you dislike?

- The Sibling Relationship -

Are you the oldest child, middle child, or the youngest child in your family? What advantages or disadvantages do you feel this gave you?

- The Sibling Relationship -

What do you feel we have in common with each other?

How do you feel we are different?

- The Sibling Relationship -

What is your favorite memory of us?

- The Sibling Relationship -

What is your favorite thing to do when we spend time together?

- The Sibling Relationship -

What is a habit that a sibling has that you would love to change?

- The Sibling Relationship -

What sets you apart from your brothers / sisters?

- The Sibling Relationship -

At what point in our relationship do you feel we were the closest?

- The Sibling Relationship -

What do you feel was the most difficult time period in our relationship?

- The Sibling Relationship -

Were you ever upset with me or disagree with something I did but stayed quiet about it?

- The Sibling Relationship -

Is there anything about our relationship that you would like to be different?

- The Sibling Relationship -

What is something about yourself that you have never told me before?

- The Sibling Relationship -

Finish this sentence:
"Remember the time when we…"

- The Sibling Relationship -

Sibling Superlatives

Between you and your sibling(s), which of you is...

The most adventurous: _____

Most likely to break the rules: _____

Going to take the longest to get ready: _____

The family comedian: _____

Most likely to take a TV show WAY too seriously: _____

Most likely to bring home a stray animal: _____

The best cook: _____

The most creative: _____

Most like Mom: _____

Most like Dad: _____

Most concerned about appearances: _____

Up before the sun rises (a morning person): _____

Still up when the sun rises (a night person): _____

Most likely to sleep through an earthquake: _____

The biggest drama king/queen: _____

The most likely to cry during a movie: _____

The one who does everything at the last minute: _____

The biggest flirt: _____

Most likely to yell at the TV during sporting events: _____

Most likely to take charge in an emergency: _____

Sibling Superlatives

Between you and your sibling(s), which of you is...

The most accident prone:

Most likely to crash on your couch:

A Mommy's boy/girl:

A Daddy's boy/girl:

Always trying to save the Earth:

The most conventional:

The "free spirit":

Most likely to become famous/infamous:

The most competitive:

Most likely to always have a coffee in hand:

Always late (with no excuses):

Always early (and lets everyone know about it):

Most likely to show up when there is free food:

The beauty:

The brains:

The one always called to help with technology:

Our parents' favorite:

The best one to go to for cheering up:

The life of the party:

The first to know everything in the family:

The Real You

What has been your favorite age or stage in life so far?

- The Real You -

How would you describe yourself?
Creative? Funny? Logical?
Generous? Impulsive?

- The Real You -

Is there anything about yourself that you would change if you could? What is it and why?

- The Real You -

What are your "good habits"?
Do you have any "bad habits"?

- The Real You -

Which parent do you feel you more closely resemble? In what way?

- The Real You -

What do you think your family and friends would say is the best part of you? Would you agree?

- The Real You -

What do you wish you had done more of in your life? What do you wish you had spent less time doing?

- The Real You -

Who has inspired you throughout your life so far?

- The Real You -

What do you like the most about our generation? What do you like the least?

- The Real You -

What is something you are really good at?

- The Real You -

What is something you are really bad at?

- The Real You -

What is something material in your life that you would never want to live without?

- The Real You -

What sights, smells, or things make you feel like a child again?

- The Real You -

Tell me about an embarrassing moment in your life. How did you cope and move through it?

- The Real You -

Describe an occasion when you were proud of yourself.

- The Real You -

What is your real passion in life?

- The Real You -

What advice have our parents given that you still follow now?

- The Real You -

Are you usually a rule follower or a rule breaker? Explain.

- The Real You -

Who is someone you were really jealous of? What made you so jealous?

- The Real You -

What is the dumbest choice you feel you have ever made?

― The Real You ―

What is the smartest thing you feel you have ever done?

- The Real You -

Do you have any really weird habits or quirks?

- The Real You -

Do you have a special or unusual talent or skill?

- The Real You -

What is your greatest fear in life?

— The Real You —

If you could only choose one for yourself, would you choose intelligence or looks? Why?

- The Real You -

What is something you've kept secret from our parents? Why have you never told them?

- The Real You -

Is there anything in your past that you would like to forget but your conscience keeps reminding you of it?

- The Real You -

What do you find yourself thinking about the most?

- The Real You -

*Do you have any unfulfilled dreams?
Tell me about them.*

- The Real You -

When you need to take a break for
"self care" or "me time"
what things do you like to do?

- The Real You -

If you had to turn to one of our parents for advice, permission or help, which parent would you choose? Why?

- The Real You -

When did you begin to feel you were really an adult and not just playing the part?

- The Real You -

Do you have any disappointments or regrets? Tell me about them.

- The Real You -

Your Favorites

Food: _____

Cuisine: _____

Dessert: _____

Drink: _____

Candy: _____

Game or Sport: _____

Athlete: _____

Book: _____

Author: _____

Television Show: _____

Movie: _____

Movie Genre: _____

Actor or Actress: _____

Composer: _____

Song: _____

Singer or Band: _____

Music Genre: _____

Animal: _____

Vacation Destination: _____

Make-up Brand: _____

Your Favorites

Pastime: _____

Modern Convenience: _____

Place to Shop: _____

Gadget or Tool: _____

Flower: _____

Person in History: _____

House Style: _____

Color: _____

Artist: _____

Article of Clothing: _____

Motivational Speaker: _____

Type of Weather: _____

Way to Relax: _____

Warm Weather Activity: _____

Cold Weather Activity: _____

Season: _____

Charity: _____

Car Make & Model: _____

Thing to Collect: _____

Quote or Verse: _____

Life

What is your earliest memory?

- Life -

Did you have a nickname growing up?
How did you get that nickname?
How did you feel about it?

- Life -

Did you have a favorite bedtime story when you were a child? Do you read (or plan to read) this same story to your own children at bedtime?

- Life -

Did you have an idol or hero as a child?
Why was this particular person your favorite?
How much influence did they have on you?

- Life -

At what age did you start dreaming of and planning your future (marriage, children, house, pets)?
Tell me about your plans.

- Life -

Who or what do you remember most fondly from childhood?

- Life -

What chores were you expected to do as a child? Do you think your chores were fair when compared to everyone else's?

What is your favorite memory of your mother?

- Life -

What is your favorite memory of your father?

- Life -

Did you participate in a youth group or youth organization? How has this experience influenced your adult life?

- Life -

When you were a child or teenager, did you have any idea what path you wanted to take after high school? What influenced your decision?

- Life -

Did you receive any education or training beyond high school? What was it? Did you earn any degrees or certifications?

- Life -

What jobs have you had in your adult life?
Which one was your favorite?
Which one do you never want to do again?

- Life -

Did you serve in the military? If so, in what branch of service? For how long? What was your rank? Where were you stationed?

- Life -

What is the most memorable experience
to come from
your time in the military?

- Life -

Knowing what you know now, is there anything you wish you had learned to better prepare you for adulthood?

- Life -

Is there anything you wish you had asked our parents or grandparents? What is it and why? Is there anything you wish they had asked you?

- Life -

Tell me about the places you have traveled.

What was your favorite place to visit?

- Life -

What is your favorite vacation memory, either from your childhood or from a trip taken more recently?

- Life -

Regarding world events and politics, how do you feel the views of our parents and grandparents have influenced your own perspective?

- Life -

Have you ever done anything illegal? How old were you? What was it? If you were caught, what were the consequences?

- Life -

What are some of your worst fashion faux pas?

- Life -

What do you feel was the most important lesson our parents taught you?

- Life -

What is your favorite holiday?
What do you love about it?

- Life -

Do you have a favorite holiday tradition? What is it? How did it start?

- Life -

What organizations or groups have you belonged to as an adult? How did you become involved in them?

- Life -

Tell about a compliment you have received that has had an impact on your life.

- Life -

*Describe a difficult choice
that you have had to make in your life.
How did you reach your decision?*

- Life -

What hardships have you experienced in your life? What challenges did you face? How did you overcome those challenges?

- Life -

Who is someone from your past, alive or not,
that you would like to see again?
What things would you say or do?

- Life -

Tell me about your first crush.
Who was it? How did you know them?
Did they know you had a crush on them?

- Life -

When did you experience your first kiss?
Who was it with? Where?
What led up to it?

- Life -

In your own words, tell me what love is. Has your definition of "love" changed through the years? If so, how?

- Life -

Who was your first love?
What attracted you to this person?

- Life -

What things have you learned from the serious relationships you have been in?

- Life -

What is the most difficult relationship challenge you have faced? How were you able to overcome it?

- Life -

Tell me about the hardest breakup you've experienced. How did you heal from it?

- Life -

Have you been married?
What made you feel sure you chose
the right person to be your life partner?

- Life -

*Were you married more than once?
How do you feel those marriages
differed from each other?*

- Life -

If you have children, who would you trust to look after them or raise them if you were unable to? Why?

*Is your parenting style similar to
the way you were raised or is it different?
Is that by choice or circumstance?*

- Life -

What advice about relationships, love and marriage can you share with me?

- Life -

What social issues of today do you have the most interest in?

- Life -

What are the most significant differences you see between the world we grew up in and the world today?

- Life -

What is something you feel you would do differently if given the chance? What impact would this have had on your life?

- Life -

Have you received any special awards or recognitions? What were they? When did you receive them?

- Life -

What are some defining moments of your life?

- Life -

What do you want your family and friends to learn from your life?

- Life -

What has been the best day of your life so far?

- Life -

What goals or dreams are you working on right now?

- Life -

What are some new skills you would like to learn?

- Life -

What are you looking forward to the most at this stage in your life?

- Life -

Describe what your perfect day would be like.

- Life -

What are some of the important "life lessons" you have gathered along the way?

- Life -

How do you want to be remembered by future generations?

- Life -

Made in the USA
Monee, IL
04 November 2024